I0408746

THE DIRECTOR

July 15, 2016

M-16-17

MEMORANDUM TO THE HEADS OF EXECUTIVE DEPARTMENTS AND AGENCIES

FROM: Shaun Donovan
            Director

SUBJECT: OMB Circular No. A-123, Management's Responsibility for Enterprise Risk
            Management and Internal Control

The Administration has emphasized the importance of having appropriate risk management processes and systems to identify challenges early, to bring them to the attention of Agency leadership, and to develop solutions. To that end, the Office of Management and Budget (OMB) is updating this Circular to ensure Federal managers are effectively managing risks an Agency faces toward achieving its strategic objectives and arising from its activities and operations. These expanded responsibilities reinforce the purposes of the Federal Managers' Financial Integrity Act (FMFIA) and the Government Performance and Results Act Modernization Act (GPRAMA), and support the Administration's commitment to improve the efficiency and effectiveness of Government.

Since 1981, OMB Circular No. A-123 (A-123) and FMFIA have been at the center of Federal requirements to improve accountability in Federal programs and operations. Over the years, government operations have changed dramatically, becoming increasingly complex and driven by changes in technology. At the same time, resources are constrained and stakeholders expect greater program integrity, efficiency and transparency into government operations.

The policy changes in this Circular modernize existing efforts by requiring agencies to implement an Enterprise Risk Management (ERM) capability coordinated with the strategic planning and strategic review process established by GPRAMA, and the internal control processes required by FMFIA and Government Accountability Office (GAO)'s Green Book. This integrated governance structure will improve mission delivery, reduce costs, and focus corrective actions towards key risks. Implementation of this policy will engage all agency management, beyond the traditional ownership of OMB Circular No. A-123 by the Chief Financial Officer community. In particular, it will require leadership from the agency Chief Operating Officer and Performance Improvement Officer, and close collaboration across all agency mission and mission-support functions.

Successful implementation of this Circular requires Agencies to establish and foster an open, transparent culture that encourages people to communicate information about potential risks and other concerns with their superiors without fear of retaliation or blame. Similarly, agency managers, Inspectors General (IG) and other auditors should establish a new set of parameters encouraging the free flow of information about agency risk points and corrective measure adoption. An open and transparent culture results in the earlier identification of risk, allowing the opportunity to develop a collaborative response, ultimately leading to a more resilient government.

This revision of the Circular has gone through an extensive deliberative process with Agencies and their IG teams, and including consultation with the GAO and many outside groups who seek more efficient and effective delivery of governmental services. This revised Circular is effective for Fiscal Year (FY) 2016 and supersedes all previous versions. Appendices A, B, C, and D of OMB Circular No. A-123 remain in effect. Updates to the GAO greenbook are effective for FY 2016. ERM implementation requirements are effective for FY 2017. OMB plans to work closely with the President's Management Council, Executive Councils, and the Council of Inspectors General on Integrity and Efficiency (CIGIE) to provide further implementation guidance.

Attachment:

OMB Circular No. A-123, Management's Responsibility for Enterprise Risk Management and Internal Control

OMB Circular No. A-123, Management's Responsibility for Enterprise Risk Management and Internal Control

Purpose: This Circular defines management's responsibilities for enterprise risk management (ERM) and internal control. The Circular provides updated implementation guidance to Federal managers to improve accountability and effectiveness of Federal programs as well as mission-support operations through implementation of ERM practices and by establishing, maintaining, and assessing internal control effectiveness. The Circular emphasizes the need to integrate and coordinate risk management and strong and effective internal control into existing business activities and as an integral part of managing an Agency.

Authority: This Circular is issued under the authority of the Federal Managers' Financial Integrity Act (FMFIA) of 1982 as codified in 31 U.S.C. 3512, and the Government Performance Results Act (GPRA) Modernization Act, Public Law 111-352.

Policy: Each Federal employee is responsible for safeguarding Federal assets and the efficient delivery of services to the public. Federal leaders and managers are responsible for establishing goals and objectives around operating environments, ensuring compliance with relevant laws and regulations, and managing both expected and unexpected or unanticipated events. They are responsible for implementing management practices that identify, assess, respond, and report on risks. Risk management practices must be forward-looking and designed to help leaders make better decisions, alleviate threats and to identify previously unknown opportunities to improve the efficiency and effectiveness of government operations. Management is also responsible for establishing and maintaining internal controls to achieve specific internal control objectives related to operations, reporting, and compliance. Management must consistently apply these internal control standards to meet the internal control principles and related components outlined in this circular and to assess and report on internal control effectiveness at least annually. Risk management practices must be taken into account when designing internal controls and assessing their effectiveness. Annually, agencies must develop a risk profile coordinated with their annual strategic reviews. Further, management must provide assurances on internal control effectiveness in its Agency Financial Report (AFR) or the Performance and Accountability Report (PAR). Information regarding identified material weaknesses and corrective actions should be included in any of the three preceding reports.

Requirements: Office of Management and Budget (OMB) Circular No. A-123 requires agencies to integrate risk management and internal control functions. The Circular also establishes an assessment process based on the Government Accountability Office's (GAO) *Standards for Internal Control in the Federal Government* (known as the Green Book) that management must implement in order to properly assess and improve internal controls over operations, reporting, and compliance. The primary compliance indicators that management must consider when implementing OMB Circular No. A-123, include:

- Management is responsible for the establishment of a governance structure to effectively implement, direct and oversee implementation of the Circular and all the provisions of a robust process of risk management and internal control.
- Implementation of the Circular should leverage existing offices or functions within the organization that currently monitor risks and the effectiveness of the organization's internal control.
- Agencies should develop a maturity model approach[1] to the adoption of an ERM framework. For FY 2016, Agencies are encouraged to develop an approach to implement ERM. For FY 2017 and thereafter Agencies must continuously build risk identification capabilities into the framework to identify new or emerging risks, and/or changes in existing risks (See Section II.C. for additional details).
- Management must evaluate the effectiveness of internal controls annually using GAO's *Standards for Internal Control in the Federal Government*. (The Green Book)

Throughout the Circular, the terms "Must" and "Will" denote a requirement that management will comply with in all cases. "Should," indicates a presumptively mandatory requirement except in circumstances where the requirement is not relevant for the Agency. "May" or "Could," indicate best practices that may be adopted at the discretion of management.

Effective Date: This Circular is effective upon publication. Appendices A, B, C, and D of OMB Circular No. A-123 remain in effect.

Applicability: This Circular is applicable to each executive agency. All other non-executive agencies of the Federal government are encouraged to adopt the Circular.

Inquiries: Further information concerning this Circular can be obtained from the Office of Federal Financial Management (202) 395-3993 or the Office of Performance and Personnel Management, (202) 395-5670 Office of Management and Budget, Washington, DC 20503.

Copies: Copies of this Circular may be obtained from www.whitehouse.gov/omb.

---

[1] See https://www.rims.org/resources/ERM/Pages/RiskMaturityModel.aspx for an example maturity model.

Significant Revisions to OMB Circular No. A-123

Section	Revision to A-123	Purpose of Revision
Transmittal to the Circular	Changed title from OMB Circular No. A-123, Management's Responsibility for Internal Control to OMB Circular No. A-123, Management's Responsibility for Enterprise Risk Management and Internal Control	Title changed to align better with the focus of the Circular towards an enterprise risk management framework.
Restructure	Former Section I, Introduction, Section II, Standards, and Section III, Integrated Internal Control Framework restructured as described below. *Appendix A, Internal Control Over Financial Reporting (ICOFR)* removed from the body of A-123 and renamed to *Appendix A, Internal Control Over Reporting (ICOR)*	Introduce Enterprise Risk Management guidance; eliminate areas of duplication; and balance emphasis on operations, compliance, and reporting. Based on the significance of GAO *Standards for Internal Control* changes related to internal control over reporting; OMB plans to issue the prior Appendix A as a standalone document. Appendices A, B, C, and D of OMB Circular No. A-123 remain in effect.
Throughout Circular	Referenced ERM concepts and guidelines based on the Committee of Sponsoring Organizations of the Treadway Commission (COSO), International Organization for Standards (ISO) and the United Kingdom's Orange Book, *Management of Risk – Principles and Concepts.*[2]	Provide additional ERM implementation guidance.
Section I. Introduction	Changed the focus of the Introduction to illustrate management's responsibility to manage risk, the relationships between A-123 and Part 6 of A-11, *Federal Performance Framework,* and *Internal Controls and Enterprise Risk Management.*	Provide an overview of the integration of Internal Controls and Enterprise Risk Management
Section II. Establishing Enterprise Risk Management in Management Practices	Addition of a new section.	Provide for more effective risk management and internal control in the Federal Government.
Section III. Establishing and Operating an Effective Internal Control System	Addition of a new section.	Provide evaluation guidance for the new GAO Green Book.

---

[2] References to non-Federal Government entities are provided to illustrate best practices and do not signify endorsement by the Federal Government.

Section	Revision to A-123	Purpose of Revision
Section IV. Assessing Internal Control	Included a summary of updated Standards of Internal Control in the Federal Government and related documentation and assessment requirements.	Provide evaluation guidance for the new GAO Green Book.
Section V. Correcting Internal Control Deficiencies	Included minimum requirements for corrective action plans.	Emphasize root cause analysis, accountability, and collaboration with Offices of Inspectors General.
Section VI. Reporting on Internal Control	Requires a single assurance statement consistent with the original requirement of the Federal managers Financial Integrity Act (FMFIA).	Provide a risk based approach and balance emphasis between operations, reporting, and compliance internal control objectives.
Section VII. Additional Considerations	Addition of a new section.	Provide additional considerations for emerging issues including: managing privacy risks, integrating acquisition assessments with the new GAO Green Book, managing grant risks and managing Antideficiency Act risks.

TABLE OF CONTENTS

LIST OF TABLES

LIST OF FIGURES

LIST OF EXHIBITS

I. INTRODUCTION

Federal leaders and managers are responsible for establishing and achieving goals and objectives, seizing opportunities to improve effectiveness and efficiency of operations, providing reliable reporting, and maintaining compliance with relevant laws and regulations. They are also responsible for implementing management practices that effectively identify, assess, respond, and report on risks. Risks arise from a variety of external and internal environments. Examples include economic, operational, and organizational change factors, all of which would negatively impact an Agency's ability to meet goals and objectives if not resolved.

Federal leaders and managers achieve these aims through a governance structure defined through a variety of sources, including laws enacted by the Congress and numerous Executive directives and Agency policies. Most relevant to this discussion, the Federal Government's core governance processes are defined by Office of Management and Budget (OMB) budget guidance, such as OMB Circular No. A-11, which defines the processes by which the Executive Branch develops and executes Strategic Plans, compiles the President's Budget request, assembles Congressional Budget Justifications, conducts performance reviews, and issues Annual Performance Plans and Annual Performance Reports. OMB Circular No. A-123 provides guidance to Federal Managers on improving the accountability and effectiveness of Federal programs and operations by identifying and managing risks, establishing requirements to assess, correct, and report on the effectiveness of internal controls.

Enterprise Risk Management (ERM) and Internal Control are components of a governance framework. ERM as a discipline deals with identifying, assessing, and managing risks. Through adequate risk management, agencies can concentrate efforts towards key points of failure and reduce or eliminate the potential for disruptive events. Internal control is a processes effected by an entity's oversight body, management, and other personnel that provides reasonable assurance that the objectives of an entity will be achieved.

Leading international standards setters in the fields of risk management and internal control including both the Committee of Sponsoring Organizations of the Treadway Commission (COSO) and the International Organization for Standardization (ISO) incorporate internal control as part of the larger risk management process. ERM is viewed as a part of the overall governance process, and internal controls as an integral part of risk management and ERM. This relationship is depicted in the following COSO-based diagram in Figure 1.

Figure 1 The Relationship Between Internal Controls and Enterprise Risk Management

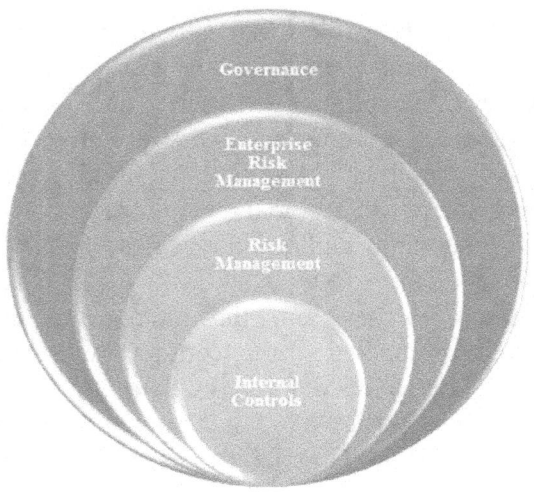

The remaining sections of this document is organized as follows:

Section II of OMB Circular No. A-123 defines management's responsibilities for ERM, and includes requirements for identifying and managing risks. Most importantly, it encourages agencies to establish a Risk Management Council (RMC), develop "Risk Profiles" which identify risks arising from mission and mission-support operations, and consider those risks as part of the annual strategic review process. It complements Section 270 of OMB Circular No. A-11, which discusses agency responsibilities for identifying and managing strategic and programmatic risk as part of agency strategic planning, performance management, and performance reporting practices. Together, these two Circulars constitute the ERM policy framework for the Federal Government, with specific ERM activities integrated and operationalized by Federal agencies.

Section III of OMB Circular No. A-123 includes guidance for establishing internal controls for those risks identified by management as requiring a formal system of internal control to provide reasonable assurance that objectives are achieved. For this subset of risks identified by management, this Circular prescribes requirements conforming with the Standards of Internal Control in the Federal Government established by the Government Accountability Office (GAO), more commonly known as the Green Book. This includes establishing and maintaining internal control to achieve specific objectives related to operations, reporting, and compliance; assessing and reporting effectiveness; and providing assurances on its Agency Financial Report (AFR), or the Performance and Accountability Report (PAR). Information regarding identified material weaknesses and corrective actions should be included in any of the three preceding reports.

Section IV of OMB Circular No. A-123 discusses management's responsibility to continuously monitor, assess, and improve the effectiveness of internal controls. Also discussed are documentation requirements, possible sources of information for use in the assessment on internal controls, identification of deficiencies and the internal control evaluation approach.

Section V of OMB Circular No. A-123 provides guidance on correcting internal control deficiencies, corrective action plan requirements and audit follow up and resolution initiatives. An Agency's corrective action process provides the ability for management to develop a plan for addressing the risk associated with a control deficiency. An Agency's ability to correct control deficiencies is an indicator of the strength of its internal control environment.

Section VI of OMB Circular No. A-123 provides guidance on annual assurance statements and reporting requirements in accordance with 31 U.S.C. 3512, (that allows for a single assurance statement), Government Corporations and classified matters. This section also provides definitions for a control deficiency, significant deficiency, and a material weakness.

Section VII of OMB Circular No. A-123 discusses additional considerations such as managing privacy risks, conducting acquisition assessments, managing risk to grants and managing Antideficiency Act risks.

II. ESTABLISHING ENTERPRISE RISK MANAGEMENT IN MANAGEMENT PRACTICES

There are several Enterprise Risk Management (ERM) models available to help organizations integrate risk management and internal control activities into a common framework. Section 270.24 of the Office of Management and Budget (OMB) Circular No. A-11 defines "risk" as the effect of uncertainty on objectives. Risk management is a series of coordinated activities to direct and control challenges or threats to achieving an organization's goals and objectives. ERM is an effective Agency-wide approach to addressing the full spectrum of the organization's external and internal risks by understanding the combined impact of risks as an interrelated portfolio, rather than addressing risks only within silos. ERM provides an enterprise-wide, strategically-aligned portfolio view of organizational challenges that provides better insight about how to most effectively prioritize resource allocations to ensure successful mission delivery. While agencies cannot respond to all risks related to achieving strategic objectives and performance goals, they must identify, measure, and assess risks related to mission delivery. Effective risk management:

- creates and protects value;
- is an integral part of all organizational processes;
- is part of decision-making;
- explicitly addresses uncertainty;
- is systematic, structured, and timely;
- is based on the best available information;
- is tailored and responsive to the evolving risk profile of the Agency;
- takes human and cultural factors into account;
- is transparent and inclusive;
- is dynamic, iterative, and responsive to change; and
- facilitates continual improvement of the organization.

ERM reflects forward-looking management decisions and balancing risks and returns so an Agency enhances its value to the taxpayer and increases its ability to achieve its strategic objectives. The Committee of Sponsoring Organizations of the Treadway Commission (COSO) ERM framework also includes the concepts of risk appetite, risk tolerance, and portfolio view:

- *Risk appetite-* is the broad-based amount of risk an organization is willing to accept in pursuit of its mission/vision. It is established by the organization's most senior level leadership and serves as the guidepost to set strategy and select objectives.

- *Risk tolerance-* is the acceptable level of variance in performance relative to the achievement of objectives. It is generally established at the program, objective or component level. In setting risk tolerance levels, management considers the relative importance of the related objectives and aligns risk tolerance with risk appetite.

- A *portfolio view of risk-* provides insight into all areas of organizational exposure to risk (such as reputational, programmatic performance, financial, information technology, acquisitions, human capital, etc.), thus increasing an Agency's chances of experiencing fewer unanticipated outcomes and executing a better assessment of risk associated with changes in the environment.

ERM is beneficial since it addresses a fundamental organizational issue: the need for information about major risks to flow both up and down the organization and across its organizational structures to improve the quality of decision-making. ERM seeks to open channels of communication so that managers have access to the information they need to make sound decisions. ERM seeks to encompass the range of major risks that threatens agencies' ability to implement their missions, programs, and operations. Most agencies should build their capabilities, first to conduct more effective risk management, then to implement ERM, rating those risks in terms of impact, and finally building internal controls to monitor and assess the risk developments at various time points. To complete this circle of risk management the Agencies must incorporate risk awareness into the agencies' culture and ways of doing business. While there are many approaches that can be taken to implement ERM, most include the following elements:[3]

---

[3] Based on The Orange Book, Management of Risk – Principles and Concepts, October 2004, HM Treasury.

Figure 2 Illustrative Example of an Enterprise Risk Management Model

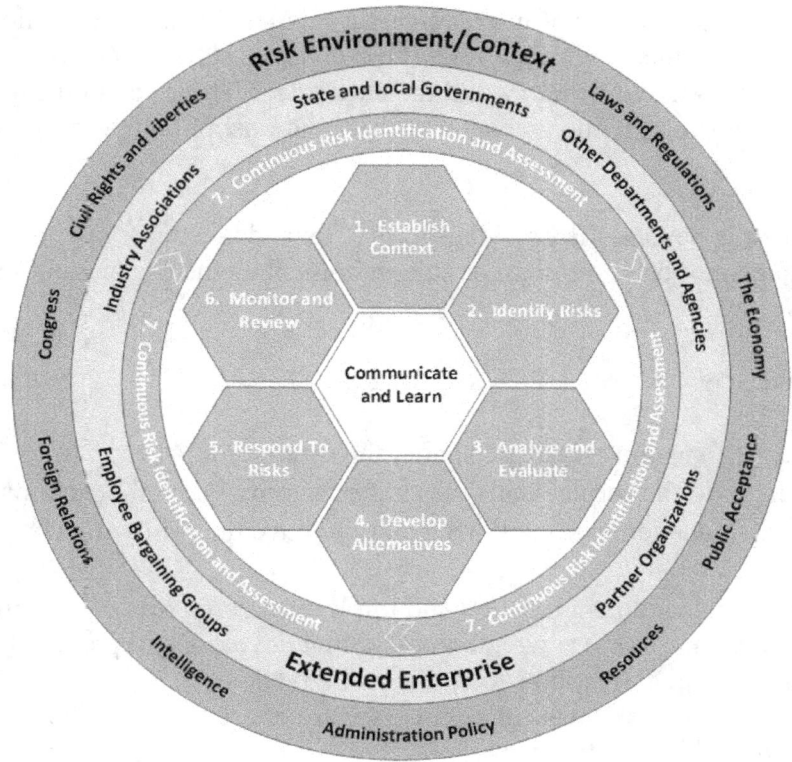

1. ***Establish the Context-***   understanding and articulating the internal and external environments of the organization.

2. ***Initial Risk Identification-***   using a structured and systematic approach to recognizing where the potential for undesired outcomes or opportunities can arise.

3. ***Analyze and Evaluate Risks-***   considering the causes, sources, probability of the risk occurring, the potential positive or negative outcomes, and then prioritizing the results of the analysis.

4. ***Develop Alternatives-***   systematically identifying and assessing a range of risk response options guided by risk appetite.

5. ***Respond to Risks-***   making decisions about the best options(s) among a number of alternatives, and then preparing and executing the selected response strategy.

6. ***Monitor and Review-***   evaluating and monitoring performance to determine whether the implemented risk management options achieved the stated goals and objectives.

7. ***Continuous Risk Identification-***   must be an iterative process, occurring throughout the year to include surveillance of leading indicators of future risk from internal and external environments.

The "extended enterprise" consists of interdependent relationships, parent-child relationships, and relationships external to an Agency. Thus, no Agency is self-contained, and risk drivers can arise out of organizations that extend beyond the enterprise. These relationships give rise to a need for assurance that risk is being managed in that relationship both appropriately and as planned.

The risk environment is beyond the boundary of the "extended enterprise." The environment generates risks that cannot be controlled, or constrain the way the organization is permitted to take on or address risk.

A. Governance

The responsibilities of managing risks are shared throughout the Agency from the highest levels of executive leadership to the service delivery staff executing Federal programs. Industry best practices suggest risk management functions generally have the following characteristics:

- helping senior management develop and implement core policies and procedures with respect to enterprise risk management, including developing a process to define risk appetite, and establish risk thresholds accordingly;
- ensuring the current risk levels and processes are consistent with the established risk tolerance thresholds and policies;
- supporting implementation of effective controls;
- developing strong reporting systems and analysis that incorporate quantitative and qualitative information to provide effective portfolio views of risk;
- identifying emerging risks, concentrations of risk, and other situations that could be properly assessed; and
- elevating critical issues to appropriate levels within an Agency in a timely fashion.

To provide governance for the risk management function, agencies may use a Risk Management Council (RMC) to oversee the establishment of the Agency's risk profile, regular assessment of risk, and development of appropriate risk response. RMC structures will vary by Agency, and in some cases may be integrated with existing management structures. An effective RMC will include senior officials for program operations and mission-support functions to help ensure those risks are identified which have the most significant impact on the mission outcomes of the Agency. Should agencies choose to use an RMC, the RMC should be chaired by the Agency Chief Operating Officer (COO) or a senior official with responsibility for the enterprise. In cabinet-level Agencies this is the Deputy Secretary.

To support this work, some agency governance structures are beginning to include a Chief Risk Officer (CRO), or equivalent function who champion agency-wide efforts to manage risk within the Agency and advise senior leaders on the strategically-aligned portfolio view of risks at the Agency. A CRO may serve as a strategic advisor to the COO and other staff on the integration of enterprise risk management practices into the day-to-day business operations and decision-making. CROs generally work with business unit managers within their organizations to identify issues in a timely manner to allow for proactive management of the program and to facilitate informed, data-driven decision-making.

Regardless of the governance structure developed, agency governance should include a process for considering risk appetite and tolerance levels. The concept of "risk appetite" is key to achieving effective ERM, and is essential to consider in determining risk responses. Although a formally documented risk appetite statement is not required, agencies must have a solid understanding of their risk appetite and tolerance levels in order to create a comprehensive enterprise-level risk profile. Risk appetite can be considered qualitatively and/or quantitatively and should be factored into the process of balancing risks with opportunities. Additionally, risk appetite and tolerance levels should be evaluated on a regular basis and adjusted accordingly to meet the needs of the organization.

See OMB Circular No. A-11 Section 270.26, for a discussion of the broader risk management roles the RMC should fulfill with respect to strategic reviews.

B. Risk Profiles[4]

Agencies must maintain a risk profile. The primary purpose of a risk profile is to provide a thoughtful analysis of the risks an Agency faces toward achieving its strategic objectives arising from its activities and operations, and to identify appropriate options for addressing significant risks. The risk profile assists in facilitating a determination around the aggregate level and types of risk that the agency and its management are willing to assume to achieve its strategic objectives. The risk profile differs from a risk register in that it is a prioritized inventory of the most significant risks identified and assessed through the risk assessment process versus a complete inventory of risks. The risk profile must consider risks from a portfolio perspective and be approved by an Agency's RMC or equivalent. Additionally, the profile must identify sources of uncertainty, both positive (opportunities) and negative (threats).

The development of an Agency risk profile:

- encourages open and candid conversations about risks facing an organization at all levels;
- facilitates the ranking of risk priorities (in particular to identify and escalate the most significant risks of which senior management should be aware);
- captures the reasons for decisions made about risk tolerances;
- facilitates recording of the way in which it is decided to address risk;
- allows leadership at all levels to understand the overall risk profile and how their areas of particular responsibility fit into it; and
- facilitates the review and regular monitoring of risks.

---

[4] Based on The Orange Book, Management of Risk – Principles and Concepts, October 2004, HM Treasury.

Agencies have discretion in terms of the appropriate content and format for their risk profiles; however, in general risk profiles should include the following seven components:

1. Identification of Objectives
2. Identification of Risk
3. Inherent Risk Assessment
4. Current Risk Response
5. Residual Risk Assessment
6. Proposed Risk Response
7. Proposed Action Category

Each of these seven components is illustrated in the table below, and further descriptions of each component, including guidance for each, follows the table. In completing their risk profiles, Agencies may consider reviewing and incorporating results from existing documentation such as GAO and OIG Audit Findings, OIG's Annual Report on Top Performance and Management Challenges, FFMIA/FMFIA documentation, Employee Viewpoint Survey Results, external media, etc.

Agencies should adhere to the general guidance provided for these components when making modifications to the content and format of their risk profiles. See Sections C1 though C7 following the table below.

Table 1 Illustrative Example of a Risk Profile

STRATEGIC OBJECTIVE – Improve Program Outcomes								
Risk	**Inherent Assessment**		**Current Risk Response**	**Residual Assessment**		**Proposed Risk Response**	**Owner**	**Proposed Risk Response Category**
	Impact	Likelihood		Impact	Likelihood			
Agency X may fail to achieve program targets due to lack of capacity at program partners.	High	High	REDUCTION: Agency X has developed a program to provide program partners technical assistance	High	Medium	Agency X will monitor capacity of program partners through quarterly reporting from partners	Primary – Program Office	Primary – Strategic Review
OPERATIONS OBJECTIVE – Manage This Risk of Fraud in Federal Operations								
Contract and Grant fraud.	High	Medium	REDUCTION: Agency X has developed procedures to ensure contract performance is monitored and that proper checks and balances are in place.	High	Medium	Agency X will provide training on fraud awareness, identification, prevention, and reporting.	Primary – Contracting or Grants Officer	Primary – Internal Control Assessment
REPORTING OBJECTIVE – Provide Reliable External Financial Reporting								
RISK	**Inherent Assessment**		**Risk Response**	**Residual Assessment**		**Proposed Action**	**Owner**	**Proposed Action Category**
	Impact	Likelihood		Impact	Likelihood			
Agency X identified material weaknesses in internal control.	High	High	REDUCTION: Agency X has developed corrective actions to provide program partners technical assistance.	High	Medium	Agency X will monitor corrective actions in consultation with OMB to maintain audit opinion.	Primary – Chief Financial Officer	Primary – Internal Control Assessment
COMPLIANCE OBJECTIVE – Comply with the Improper Payments Legislation								
Program X is highly susceptible to significant improper payments.	High	High	REDUCTION: Agency X has developed corrective actions to ensure improper payment rates are monitored and reduced.	High	Medium	Agency X will develop budget proposals to strengthen program integrity.	Primary – Program Office	Primary – Internal Control Assessment and Strategic Review

B1.   Identification of Objectives

Risk must be analyzed in relation to achievement of the strategic objectives established in the Agency strategic plan (See OMB Circular No. A-11, Section 230), as well as risk in relation to appropriate operational objectives. Specific objectives must be identified and documented to facilitate identification of risks to strategic, operations, reporting, and compliance. This process assists in the identification of formal internal controls and compliance with the FMFIA, as discussed in Section III. In summary, the risk profile must include the following objectives:

- **Strategic Objectives:** relating to the strategic goals and objectives aligned with and supporting the Agency's Mission (See OMB Circular No. A-11, Section 230).

- **Operations Objectives:** relating to the effective and efficient use of the Agency's resources related to administrative and major program operations, including financial and fraud objectives (Refer to Section III, Establishing And Operating An Effective System Of Internal Control).

- **Reporting Objectives:** relating to the reliability of the Agency's reporting.

- **Compliance Objectives:** relating to the Agency's compliance with applicable laws and regulations.

In some cases there will be overlap across these categories, and agencies have discretion in terms of how to address this overlap. In addition, Agencies may find it useful to include additional subcategories of one or more objectives categories to facilitate communication on a narrower topic. One of the most common subcategories includes reputational risk. Reputational risk damages the reputation of an Agency or component of an Agency to the point of having a detrimental effect capable of affecting the Agency's ability to carry out mission objectives. Examples of reputational risk include the loss of confidence and trust, which stakeholders have in an organization to deliver operational services, or the loss of an Agency's financial statement opinion. Agencies may use their discretion in determining how to incorporate additional subcategories into their risk profile.

B2.   Identification of Risk

Identifying risks is a critical step in building the Agency's risk profile. The identification of risk can be separated into two distinct phases:

1. Initial risk identification (for an Agency which has not previously identified its risks in a structured way, or for a new component of an Agency, or perhaps for a new project or activity within an Agency); and

2. Continuous risk identification (which is necessary to identify new or emerging risks, and/or changes in existing risks).

The identification of risk is a continuous and ongoing process. Once initial risks are identified, it is important to re-examine risks on a regular basis to identify new risks or changes to existing risks.

Assessing risk is the next critical step in building the Agency's risk profile, which includes three important principles:

1. Ensure that there is a clearly structured process in which both likelihood and impact are considered for each risk;

2. record the assessment of risk in a way which facilitates monitoring and the identification of risk priorities; and

3. be clear about the difference between inherent and residual risk.

Some risk is unavoidable and beyond an organization's ability to reduce to a tolerable level. Nevertheless, the organization should make contingency plans and manage risks against those plans. For example, many organizations have to accept that risk arises due to natural disaster situations that they cannot control.

B3. Inherent Risk Assessment

Inherent risk is the exposure arising from a specific risk before any action has been taken to manage it beyond normal operations. The impact on the Agency's ability to achieve its objectives if the risk occurred can be ranked by appropriate categories, as can the likelihood that each significant risk might occur. While agencies can design their own appropriate categories, for the purposes of this guidance the following illustrative definitions can be used:

Impact

- High: the impact could preclude or highly impair the entity's ability to achieve one or more of its objectives or performance goals;
- Medium: the impact could significantly affect the entity's ability to achieve one or more of its objectives or performance goals; and
- Low: the impact will not significantly affect the entity's ability to achieve one or more of its objectives or performance goals.

Likelihood

- High: the risk is very likely or reasonably expected to occur;
- Medium: the risk is more likely to occur than unlikely; and
- Low: the risk is unlikely to occur.

B4. Current Risk Response

The action taken to manage the risk. It could involve one or more of the following:

- **Acceptance:** No action is taken to respond to the risk based on the insignificance of the risk; or the risk is knowingly assumed to seize an opportunity.

- **Avoidance:** Action is taken to stop the operational process, or the part of the operational process, causing the risk.

- **Reduction:** Action is taken to reduce the likelihood or impact of the risk.

- **Sharing:** Action is taken to transfer or share risks across the entity or with external parties, such as insuring against losses.[5]

Risk responses take many forms, including: avoidance of risk by development of a legislative proposal; reduction of risk by proposing to increase funding for the activity; acceptance of the risk of adopting a new technology in order to provide better services to customers. Formulation of risk responses should consider the organization's risk appetite and tolerance levels. The development of risk responses should be used to inform decision-making through existing management processes including the strategic reviews, development of the legislative and policy agenda, operational planning, and budget formulation.

As part of developing the risk profile, management must determine those risks for which the appropriate response includes implementation of formal internal control activities as described in Section III of this guidance and which conform to the standards published by GAO in the Green Book. These include those risks that meet each of the following criteria:

- The Agency is working to reduce exposure to the risk.
- The objective is related to reporting, compliance, or operations, including both administrative operations and the major operational components of programs.
- The risk is identified in the Agency risk profile as at least medium impact and medium likelihood (i.e., the risk is greater than low).
- Public reporting on the risk will not negatively impact services provided to the public, national security, or agency operations.
- Control objectives can be clearly specified.

---

[5] Based on definitions outlined by GAO in the Green Book.

B5. Residual Risk Assessment

Residual risk is the exposure remaining from an inherent risk after action has been taken to manage it, using the same assessment standards as the inherent assessment.

B6. Proposed Action

Additional action proposed to further reduce the exposure remaining after the risk mitigation actions have been taken, for consideration by senior management, Proposed risk responses should use the same standards applied to the current risk response, as described above, including the identification of risks for which implementation of formal internal control activities is appropriate.

B7. Proposed Risk Response Category

Identification of the existing management process that will be used to implement and monitor proposed actions. Those proposed actions that will be discussed with OMB as part of the annual Strategic Review must be identified (See OMB Circular No. A-11, Section 270), as well as proposed actions to be considered during formulation of the President's Budget. In particular, the RMC or other equivalent governance body, must categorize actions for the adoption of formal internal control activities (as described in Section III of this guidance and which conform to the standards published by GAO in the Green Book), when the criteria identified above under Current Risk Responses have been met.

Risk Profile Disclosure. As explained above, the development of agency risk profiles requires candor, subjective evaluations, and frank discussions in identifying the likelihood and severity of internal vulnerabilities. In addition, risk profiles serve to inform the development of agency strategic plans as well as the President's Budget. As such, agency risk profiles will often contain pre-decisional, deliberative, confidential, or sensitive information. Agencies are encouraged to consult with their Office of General Counsel if there are questions regarding the disclosure of such information.

C. Implementation

The management of risk must be regularly reviewed to monitor whether or not the risk profile has changed and to gain assurance that risk management is effective or if further action is necessary. In addition, processes must be put in place to review whether risks still exist, whether new risks have arisen, whether the likelihood and impact of risks have changed, to report significant changes that adjust risk priorities, and deliver assurance on the effectiveness of control. In addition, the overall risk management process must be subjected to regular review to deliver assurance that it remains appropriate and effective. At a minimum, management's risk management review processes must[6]:

- ensure that all aspects of the risk management process are reviewed at least once a year;
- ensure that risks themselves are subjected to review with appropriate frequency; and
- make provisions for alerting the appropriate level of management to new or emerging risks, as well as changes in already identified risks, so that the change can be appropriately addressed.

Federal agencies have diverse missions, and are at different levels of maturity in terms of their capacity to fully implement ERM. The Agency's approach for developing risk profiles and implementing ERM should be refined and improved each year. This guidance recognizes that not all components of an ERM process are fully operationalized in the initial years, and agency leadership must set priorities in terms of implementation. Unless otherwise approved by OMB, agencies must meet the following deadlines:

Figure 3 ERM Development and Implementation Deadlines

Deliverable	Due Date – No later than:	Description
ERM Implementation Approach	*As soon as practicable, prior to June Initial Risk Profile deliverable*	Agencies are encouraged (not required) to develop an approach to implement Enterprise Risk Management (ERM) which may include: • planned risk management governance structure, • Process for considering risk appetite and risk tolerance levels, • methodology for developing a risk profile, • general implementation timeline, and plan for maturing the comprehensiveness and quality of the risk profiles over time.
Initial Risk Profile	*June 2, 2017**	Agencies must complete their initial risk profiles in coordination with the agency Strategic Reviews. Key findings should be made available for discussion with OMB by June 2, 2017* as part of the Agency Strategic Review meetings and/or FedSTAT. The final determination on information to be shared with OMB will be provided in early 2017. This initial Risk Profile will inform the development of each Agency's new strategic plan and the President's FY 2019 Budget.
Integration with Management Evaluation of Internal Control	*September 15, 2017*	For those risks for which formal internal controls have been identified as part of the Initial Risk Profile in FY 2017, all agencies must present assurances on internal control processes in the FY 2017 Agency Financial Report (AFR) or the Performance and Accountability Report (PAR), along with a report on identified material

---

[6] Based in part on The Orange Book, Management of Risk – Principles and Concepts, October 2004, HM Treasury.

		weaknesses and corrective actions. Until an agency has fully implemented an ERM approach to risk management, it may continue to provide the existing risk assurance statements to their OIG and/or private accounting firms, as appropriate.
Updated Risk Profile	*Annually by June 3**	No less than annually, all agencies must prepare a complete risk profile and include required risk components and elements required by this guidance. CFO Act agencies, at a minimum, must complete their risk profiles in coordination with the agency Strategic Review. For these Agencies, key findings should be made available for discussion with OMB by June 3rd* as part of the agency Strategic Review meetings and/or FedStat. The final determination on information to be shared with OMB will be provided in advance of these discussions. The Risk Profile will help to inform changes to strategy, policy, operations, and the President's Budget.

* OMB Circular No. A-11, Part 6, is the authoritative policy guidance on deadlines for the Summary of Findings from the agency Strategic Reviews, including the timing of submissions to OMB. Agencies should consult OMB Circular No. A-11 as each prepares materials.

After initial implementation, the agency's risk profile must be discussed each year with OMB as a component of the summary of findings from the Agency strategic review and FedSTAT (See OMB Circular No. A-11, Section 270). For those objectives for which formal internal control activities have been identified as part of the Risk Profile, assurances on internal control processes must be presented in the Agency Financial Report (AFR) or Performance and Accountability Report (PAR), along with a report on identified material weaknesses and corrective actions.

D. Role of Auditors in Enterprise Risk Management

Management is responsible for Enterprise Risk Management systems. Internal or external auditors conduct independent and objective audits, evaluations, and investigations of an Agency's programs and operations, which includes aspects of the internal control and risk management systems. Management uses the results of such evaluations, including accompanying findings and recommendations, to monitor the design or operating effectiveness of these systems at a specific time or of a specific function or process. Auditors are also responsible for keeping management informed about risks that it detects, including fraud risks, and thereby provides information to management for use in the identification and assessment of risks. Management and external auditors might have different interpretations of risks based on their respective roles and responsibilities. The agency risk function should seek to coordinate their roles so that the independence and scope of the external auditor's role is preserved while ensuring the continuing flow of risk information to the risk management function.

III. ESTABLISHING AND OPERATING AN EFFECTIVE SYSTEM OF INTERNAL CONTROL

The FMFIA requires the GAO to prescribe standards of internal control in the Federal Government, more commonly known as the Green Book. These standards provide the internal control framework and criteria Federal managers must use in designing, implementing, and operating an effective system of internal control. The Green Book defines internal control as a process effected by an entity's oversight body, management, and other personnel that provides reasonable assurance that the objectives of an entity are achieved. These objectives and related risks can be broadly classified into one or more of the following categories:

- Operations: Effectiveness and efficiency of operations;
- Reporting: Reliability of reporting for internal and external use; and
- Compliance: Compliance with applicable laws and regulations.

A subset of the categories of objectives are the safeguarding of all assets. Management designs an internal control system to provide reasonable assurance regarding the prevention or prompt detection and correction of unauthorized acquisition, use, or disposition of an entity's assets.

FMFIA also requires OMB, in consultation with GAO, to establish guidelines for agencies to evaluate their systems of internal control to determine FMFIA compliance. Instead of considering internal control as an isolated management tool, agencies must integrate their efforts to meet the requirements of the FMFIA with the Enterprise Risk Management (ERM) requirements discussed in Section II. Thus, internal control is an integral part of the entire cycle of strategic planning, goal and objective setting, budgeting, program management, accounting, and auditing. It must support the effectiveness and the integrity of every step of the process and provide continual feedback to management.

Federal managers must carefully consider the appropriate balance between risk, controls, costs, and benefits in their mission-support operations. Too many controls can result in inefficiencies, while too few controls might increase risk to an unacceptable level.

Management's responsibility is to develop and maintain effective internal control that is consistent with its established risk appetite and risk tolerance levels. In addition, management is responsible for establishing and integrating internal control into its operations in a risk-based and cost beneficial manner, in order to provide reasonable assurance that the entity's internal control over operations, reporting, and compliance is operating effectively.

Achieving the objectives of external reporting and compliance, which are based largely on laws, rules, regulations, and standards established by Congress, GAO, and OMB, depends on how activities within the Agency's control are performed. Generally, management and oversight bodies have greater discretion in setting internal reporting objectives that are not driven by external parties. However, Agency's may choose to align its internal and external reporting objectives to allow internal reporting to better support the Agency's external reporting.

Achievement of some operations objectives – such as certain aspects of program outcomes or maintaining safe operations – are not always within the Agency's control. An effective internal control system increases the likelihood that an entity achieves its objectives. However, no matter how well designed, implemented, or operated, an internal control system cannot provide absolute assurance that all of an organization's objectives are met. Factors outside the control or influence of management can affect the entity's ability to achieve all of its objectives. For example, a natural disaster can affect an organization's ability to achieve its objectives. Therefore, once in place, effective internal control provides reasonable, not absolute, assurance that an organization achieves its objectives.

The Green Book is organized by five components of internal control as shown in the exhibit below. In addition, the five components of internal control contain 17 required principles and each principle has important attributes which explain the principles in greater detail.

Table 2 Summary of Green Book Components and Principles of Internal Control

Components of Internal Control	Principles
Control Environment	1. Demonstrate Commitment to Integrity and Ethical Values 2. Exercise Oversight Responsibility 3. Establish Structure, Responsibility and Authority 4. Demonstrate Commitment to Competence 5. Enforce Accountability
Risk Assessment	6. Define Objectives and Risk Tolerances 7. Identify, Analyze, and Respond to Risk 8. Assess Fraud Risk 9. Analyze and Respond to Change
Control Activities	10. Design Control Activities 11. Design Activities for Information Systems 12. Implement Control Activities
Information and Communication	13. Use Quality Information 14. Communicate Internally 15. Communicate Externally
Monitoring	16. Perform Monitoring Activities 17. Remediate Deficiency

Federal managers must carefully consider the appropriate balance between controls and risk in their programs and operations. To emphasize, too many controls can result in inefficient and ineffective government; agency managers must ensure an appropriate balance between the strength of controls and the relative risk associated with particular programs and operations. The benefits of controls should outweigh the cost. Agencies should consider both qualitative and quantitative factors when analyzing costs against benefits.

A. Governance.

Agencies must have a Senior Management Council (SMC) to assess and monitor deficiencies in internal control. This SMC may be a subset of the Risk Management Council, however, agencies have discretion in determining the appropriate structure. A Senior Management Council may include the Chief Financial Officer, Chief Human Capital Officer, Chief Information Officer, Chief Information Security Officer, Chief Acquisition Officer, Senior

Agency Official for Privacy, Designated Agency Ethics Official, and Performance Improvement Officer and the managers of other program offices, must be involved in identifying and ensuring correction of systemic material weaknesses relating to their respective programs. Such councils generally recommend to the Agency head which significant deficiencies are deemed to be material weaknesses to the Agency as a whole, and must therefore be included in the annual FMFIA assurance statement and reported in the Agency's Annual Financial Report (AFR) or Performance Accountability Report (PAR). This council should be responsible for overseeing the timely implementation of corrective actions related to material weaknesses. Such a council is also useful in determining when sufficient action has been taken to declare that a significant deficiency or material weakness has been corrected (though the final official determination likely resides with the Agency Head and the OIG). The SMC should also include Senior Assessment Teams to lead assessments related to the objective of internal control over reporting (See Appendix A to OMB Circular No. A-123, *Internal Control Over Reporting*).

B. Establish Entity Level Control

Establishing Entity Level Control (ELC) is another primary step in operating an effective system of internal control. The Green Book defines ELCs as controls that have a pervasive effect on an entity's internal control system and pertain to multiple components. ELCs are mostly within the Control Environment, Risk Assessment, Information and Communication, and Monitoring components of the Green Book. Control Activities are also considered a component of ELC and provide a link to an Agency's processes as described in Section C below. Entity-level controls also include controls related to the entity's use of service organizations or management override of internal control and fraud.

B1. Service Organizations

The Green Book provides internal control considerations for service organizations (shared service providers (SSP) are one example). Service organization internal control considerations include management's responsibility for the performance of third party provided processes, establishing "user controls" at the Agency receiving services, and service organization oversight.

- **Management's Responsibility for the Processes Performed by Third Party Service Organizations.** Third party service providers perform activities for many agencies. Examples include, but are not limited to: accounting and payroll processing, employee benefit plan servicing, information technology services, protections for sensitive Agency data, acquisition or procurement services, security services, asset management, health care claims processing, and loan servicing. Agencies are ultimately responsible for the services and processes provided by third party service organizations as they relate to the Agency's ability to maintain internal control over operations, reporting, and compliance with laws and regulations.
- **Management's Responsibility for Establishing User Controls.** If the processes provided by the third party service organization is significant to an Agency's internal control objectives, then the Agency is responsible for establishing user Agency controls that complement the service organization's controls. Management still

retains overall responsibility and accountability for all controls related to the processes provided by the third party, and must monitor the process as a whole to make sure it is effective. Examples of user Agency controls include:

- **Input/ Output Controls:** In most third party provider situations, the Agency must have access to the information processed by a service organization. In some cases, this information enables the Agency to compare the service organization's results with the results of an independent source. For example, an Agency using a payroll service organization compares the data submitted to the service organization with reports or information received from the service organization after the data has been processed.

- **Performance Monitoring:** Agencies must have a process for monitoring the service organization's performance in relation to various metrics, as typically defined in a service-level agreement. Most of these metrics must be tailored to specific operations. For example, agencies regularly review the security, availability, and processing integrity of service-level agreements.

- **Process Controls:** In some third party provider situations, the Agency's user controls are closely tied to the service organization's processes and provide direct assurance over their operation. For example, an Agency that has its IT development provided by a third party service organization chooses to document, track, approve, and test all application changes internally, thus retaining significant control over the IT development process.

- **Management's Responsibility for Oversight of Service Organizations.** The extent of an Agency's oversight of a service organization depends on the nature of the contract or agreement terms and conditions. The use of a third party provider needs to be considered for management's oversight and assessment of internal control based on risk and when the activity is significant to the Agency's achievement of internal control objectives of operations, reporting, or compliance. Examples of services provided by the service organization that warrant oversight include: maintenance of a user Agency's financial reporting and accounting records; safeguarding of a user Agency's assets; services that involve personally identifiable information (PII); investments for employee benefit plans; mortgage services from servicers that service mortgages for others; or application services for technology environments that support operations.

- **Service Organization Responsibility.** Service Organizations are responsible for providing assurances to their customers and assisting customers in understanding the relationship between the service provider's controls and the customer's user controls. Together, service organizations and customers manage the risks of third party provider activities typically through a Service Organization Control (SOC) 1 Type 2

Report (more technically referred to as a Statement on Standards for Attestation Engagement No. 16 report[7]). SOC 1 report considerations include:

- o Ensuring the SOC report adequately addresses the relevant internal control objectives.
- o Determining the extent and adequacy of internal control testing performed on the operating effectiveness of internal controls throughout a specified period.
- o Ensuring the SOC Report(s) cover a substantial portion of the fiscal year and bridge or roll forward letters are considered.
- o Reviewing the SOC report opinion (e.g., Unmodified) and determining what impact any internal control deficiencies included in the SOC report have on the related control objectives.
- o Evaluating complementary user entity controls included in the SOC 1 report to determine that the appropriate controls are in place to support the activities of the service provider.
- o Considering any complementary subservice organization controls included in the SOC 1 report and the effectiveness of controls at subservice organizations.

B2. Managing Fraud Risks in Federal Programs

The Green Book defines fraud as obtaining something of value through willful misrepresentation. Whether an act is fraud is a determination to be made through the judicial or other adjudicative system and is beyond management's professional responsibility for assessing risk. Waste is the act of using or expending resources carelessly, extravagantly, or to no purpose. Abuse involves behavior that is deficient or improper when compared with behavior that a prudent person considers reasonable and necessary in operational practice given the facts and circumstances. This includes the misuse of authority or position for personal gain or for the benefit of another. Waste and abuse do not necessarily involve fraud or illegal acts. [8] Principle 8 of the Green Book requires management to consider the potential for fraud when identifying, analyzing, and responding to risks.

OMB Circular No. A-123 Fraud Risk Profile Requirements. Fraud jeopardizes Agency missions by diverting scarce resources from their intended purpose. A single case of fraud can undermine programmatic mission, disrupt services, and force management to expend valuable time, resources, and staff-hours to resolve and recover property lost due to fraud. Reputational risks of fraud can damage the perception of an Agency, impact employee morale, and create distrust by the public, further hindering their efforts to provide services to the public. To the extent that Federal managers can effectively mitigate and prevent fraud from occurring, it can

---

[7] Effective for service auditors' reports dated on or after May 1, 2017, service organization reports will be prepared under a new clarified attestation standard –AU-320.

[8] GAO Standards for Internal Control in the Federal Government, GAO-14-704G, Section 8.03. http://www.gao.gov/assets/670/665712.pdf.

save time and resources spent in investigating and prosecuting fraud, and recovering lost money and property, thus avoiding the "pay and chase model."

Management has overall responsibility for establishing internal controls to manage the risk of fraud. This includes reporting to the Agency's governance structure what actions have been taken to manage fraud risks and on the status of the Agency's Risk Profile. The Agency's Risk Profile as required by Section II of OMB Circular No. A-123 must include an evaluation of fraud risks and use a risk-based approach to design and implement financial and administrative control activities to mitigate identified material fraud risks. Refer to Appendix A of OMB Circular No. A-123, *Internal Control over Reporting*, for requirements related to reporting internal control objectives. The financial and administrative controls established through the Agency's risk profile must also include:

- controls to address identified fraud risks related to payroll, beneficiary payments, grants, large contracts, information technology and security, asset safeguards, and purchase, travel and fleet cards;
- collecting and analyzing data from reporting mechanisms on detected fraud to monitor fraud trends and using that data and information to continuously improve fraud prevention controls; and
- using the results of monitoring, evaluation, and investigations to improve fraud prevention, detection, and response.

GAO Framework for Managing Fraud Risks in Federal Programs. To help managers to combat fraud and preserve integrity in government agencies and programs, GAO identified leading practices for managing fraud risks and organized them into a conceptual framework called the Fraud Risk Management Framework (the Framework, GAO-15-593SP). Managers should adhere to these leading practices as part of their efforts to effectively design, implement, and operate an internal control system that addresses fraud risks. Managers are responsible for determining the extent to which the leading practices in the Framework are relevant to their program and for tailoring the practices, as appropriate, to align with the program's operations.

The Framework encompasses control activities to prevent, detect, and respond to fraud, with an emphasis on prevention, as well as structures and environmental factors that influence or help managers achieve their objective to mitigate fraud risks. In addition, the Framework highlights the importance of monitoring and incorporating feedback, which are ongoing practices that apply to the following four components described below.

- Commit to combating fraud by creating an organizational culture and structure conducive to fraud risk management.
- Plan regular fraud risk assessments and assess risks to determine a fraud risk profile.
- Evaluate outcomes using a risk-based approach and adapt activities to improve fraud risk management.
- Design and implement a strategy with specific control activities to mitigate assessed fraud risks and collaborate to help ensure effective implementation.

Establishing Risk Tolerances in Disaster Situations. Managers must balance their priorities to fulfill the program's mission, such as effectively disbursing funds or providing services to beneficiaries, and taking actions to safeguard taxpayer dollars from improper use. For example, in disaster situations, fraud risks are higher than under normal circumstances because the need to provide services quickly can hinder the effectiveness of existing controls and creates additional opportunities for individuals to engage in fraud. As a result, managers face additional challenges balancing their mission to provide assistance quickly with implementing controls to address the increased risk of fraud.

GAO's Fraud Framework calls for managers to determine risk tolerances when assessing fraud risks and to use that determination as part of the basis for developing responses to identified fraud risks, including specific controls to address the risks. Risk tolerance reflects managers' willingness to accept a higher level of fraud risks and vary depending on the circumstances of the program. When determining risk tolerance in disaster situations, managers weigh the program's operational objective of expeditiously providing assistance against the objective of lowering the likelihood of fraud, because activities to lower fraud risks—such as the risk that ineligible individuals submit fraudulent applications for benefits—causing delays in service. As a result, managers are willing to accept a somewhat higher risk of fraud than under normal circumstances in order to provide emergency assistance in a timely manner. GAO's Fraud Framework provides a basis for managers to make decisions about how to respond to fraud risks, including determining the specific controls to design and implement, given managers' defined risk tolerances.

Managers can find additional guidance provided in the Association of Government Accountants (AGA) Fraud Prevention Tool Kit useful when managing specific types of fraud risks in Federal programs. AGA's Fraud Prevention Tool Kit provides current, state-of-the-art tools for Federal, state, local, and tribal government financial managers to use in preventing and detecting fraud.

IV. ASSESSING INTERNAL CONTROL

Agency managers must continuously monitor, assess, and improve the effectiveness of internal control associated with those internal control objectives identified as part of their risk profile. This continuous monitoring, and other periodic evaluations, provide the basis for the Agency Head's annual assessment and report on internal control as required by the FMFIA.

A. Documentation Requirements

Agency management must determine the appropriate level of documentation needed to support this assessment. The Green Book provides documentation requirements that are a necessary part of an effective internal control system. The level and nature of documentation vary based on the size of the entity and the complexity of the operational processes the entity performs. Management uses judgment in determining the extent of documentation that is needed. Documentation is required to demonstrate the design, implementation, and operating effectiveness of an entity's internal control system. The Green Book includes minimum documentation requirements as follows:

- If management's assessment determines that a principle is not relevant, management supports that determination with documentation that includes the rationale of how, in the absence of that principle, the associated component may be designed, implemented, and operated effectively.
- Management develops and maintains documentation of its internal control system.
- Management documents in policies the internal control responsibilities of the organization.
- Management evaluates and documents the results of ongoing monitoring and separate evaluations to identify internal control issues.
- Management evaluates and documents internal control issues and determines appropriate corrective actions for internal control deficiencies on a timely basis.
- Management completes and documents corrective actions to remediate internal control deficiencies on a timely basis.

B. Sources of Information

The Agency's assessment of internal control may be documented using a variety of information sources to include:

- Management documentation of its internal control system, policies, procedures, and knowledge gained from the daily operation of Agency programs and systems.
- Management reviews conducted (i) expressly for the purpose of assessing internal control, or (ii) for other purposes with an assessment of internal control as a by-product of the review.
- Annual performance plans, reports, strategic reviews and program evaluations relevant to internal control pursuant to the *GPRA Modernization Act* and OMB Circular No. A-11, Section 200, Federal Performance Framework.

- Acquisition Assessments pursuant to OMB Memorandum: *Conducting Acquisition Assessments under OMB Circular No. A-123*, May 21, 2008.
- Management reviews and annual evaluations and reports related to information technology, information security, and information resources pursuant to the Federal Information Security Modernization Act of 2014 and OMB Circular No. A-130, *Responsibilities for Protecting Federal Information Resources.*
- Outputs of governance mechanisms for information technology resources published by the Agency, pursuant to the "CIO Authorities" described in the *Federal Information Technology Acquisition Reform Act* (FITARA).
- Office of Government Ethics Program Reviews and other internal Agency ethics program reviews.
- Annual reviews and reports pursuant to the Improper Payments Information Act of 2002, as amended by the Improper Payments Elimination and Recovery Act of 2010 and the Improper Payments Elimination and Recovery Improvement Act of 2012.
- Program reviews conducted pursuant to OMB Circular No. A-129, *Policies for Federal Credit Programs and Non-Tax Receivables.*
- Single Audit Act Reports and program reviews conducted pursuant to the *Uniform Administrative Requirements, Cost Principles, and Audit Requirements for Federal Awards* for grant-making agencies.
- Antideficiency Act Reviews and Investigations.
- Independent audit reports including Office of Inspectors General Management Challenges and GAO High Risk Reports.
- Internal audit reports.
- Reports and other information provided by the Congressional committees of jurisdiction.
- Other reviews or reports relating to Agency operations or management controls.
- Assessments of internal control over financial reporting and reviews of financial management systems pursuant to Appendix A of OMB Circular No. A-123, *Internal Control Over Reporting,* Appendix B to OMB Circular No. A-123, *Improving the Management of Government Charge Card Program,* Appendix C to OMB Circular No. A-123, *Requirements for Effective Estimation and Remediation of Improper Payments,* or Appendix D to OMB Circular No. A-123, *Compliance with the Federal Financial Management Improvement Act.*

Use of information should take into consideration the completeness of the assessment and whether the process included an evaluation of internal control. Agency management should avoid duplicating reviews that assess internal controls, and should coordinate their efforts with other evaluations to the extent practical.

C. Identification of Deficiencies

Agency managers and employees should identify deficiencies in internal control from the sources of information described above and the results of their assessment process. The assessment process must include an assessment of compliance with each of the Green Book components and principles. In addition, the identification of deficiencies must include all management and operational functions and processes that support mission delivery. Agency employees and managers report control deficiencies, at a minimum to the next supervisory level, which allows the chain of command structure to determine the relative importance of each deficiency. Reporting of deficiencies should also include reporting deficiencies to the Agency's Inspector General. Definitions of control deficiencies, significant deficiencies, and material weaknesses are provided in Section VI.

Agency managers and staff are encouraged to identify control deficiencies, as this reflects positively on the Agency's commitment to recognizing and addressing management problems. Failing to report a known material weakness or significant deficiency reflects adversely on the Agency and continue to place the Agency's mission support operations at risk. Agencies must carefully consider whether systemic weaknesses exist that adversely affect internal control across organizational or program lines.

D. Internal Control Evaluation Approach

Management is responsible for evaluating whether a system of internal control reduces the risk of not achieving the entity's objectives related to operations, reporting, or compliance to an acceptable level. In evaluating internal control, management should follow a risk-based assessment approach:[9]

1. **Conduct an Assessment of Internal Control.** Management must conduct an evaluation of internal controls for each of the Green Book's principles for each of the entity objectives.
2. **Prepare a Summary of Internal Control Deficiencies.** Management should leverage an aggregated or summary log of all identified internal control deficiencies from the sources of information listed in Section B above and the results of their assessment process. The log may support the evaluation of the Green Book's Internal Control Components and Principles.
3. **Conclude on Internal Control Principle Evaluation.** Management must summarize its determination of whether each principle is designed, implemented, and operating effectively. That determination is a function of management judgment based on:
   a. the applicability of the principle to the Agency's circumstances,
   b. whether the Agency has actually been able to implement, perform, and apply the principle,
   c. any internal control deficiency that may result,
   d. the extent of compensating internal controls within the principle, and
   e. the extent to which the remaining risk impacts on the Agency's ability to achieve its objectives and meet its mission and goals.

---

[9] Section based on COSO, Internal Control – Integrated Framework, Illustrative Tools for Assessing Effectiveness of a System of Internal Control (New York: American Institute of Certified Public Accountants, 2013).

Evaluation of whether each principle is designed, implemented, and operating effectively must be of the "yes/no" type.

4. **Conclude on Internal Control Component Evaluation.** Management must also summarize its determination of whether each component is designed, implemented, and operating effectively. Similar to item three above, evaluation of internal control components is a function of management judgment and qualitative determinations. If an internal control principle is not designed, implemented, and operating effectively, management is unable to conclude that the internal control component is operating effectively.

5. **Conclude on Overall Assessment of a System of Internal Control.** Management must summarize its determination of whether each of the Green Book's components and principles are designed, implemented, and operating effectively and components are operating together in an integrated manner. In addition, management must determine the severity of internal control deficiencies or combination of deficiencies when aggregated across the components. If one or more internal control components are not operating effectively, a material weakness must be reported.

The following table illustrates how internal control principles within the control environment component roll up into the determination of whether the component is designed, implemented, and operating effectively, in addition to the overall assessment of a system of internal control. Examples below include illustrative summaries of control deficiencies.

Table 3 Illustrative Internal Control Evaluation – Control Environment

| Illustrative Internal Control Evaluation – Control Environment ||
Principle	Control Deficiency Summary
Principle 1: Demonstrate Commitment to Integrity and Ethical Values	The Agency's ethics training program is not sufficient to make all employees aware of the importance of adhering to the executive branch employee standards of conduct.
	The Agency does not have processes in place to detect and mitigate potential employee conflicts of interest.
	Management concludes the principle is not designed, implemented, and operating effectively.
Principle 2: Exercise Oversight Responsibility	Internal control deficiency noted because the Senior Management Council's review of risk assessments and remediation plans are not documented.
	Management concludes that the principle is designed, implemented, and operating effectively despite internal control deficiencies based on an evaluation of the severity of deficiencies and that compensating controls are in place.
Principle 3: Establish Structure, Responsibility and Authority	Internal control deficiency noted because oversight and control structures have not evolved to keep up with changes in operations.
	Management concludes that the principle is designed, implemented, and operating effectively as the deficiency noted only affect a small portion of the Agency.
Principle 4: Demonstrate Commitment to Competence	No internal control deficiencies noted.
	Management concludes that the principle is designed, implemented, and operating effectively.
Principle 5: Enforce Accountability	Internal control deficiencies noted because management, with oversight from the Senior Management Council, does not take necessary corrective actions.
	Management concludes that the principle is not designed, implemented, and operating effectively.

The following table is an illustrative example of the results of management's assessment of the control environment component:

Table 4 Principle and Component Evaluation

| Principle Evaluation |||
Principle	Designed & Implemented (Yes/No)	Operating Effectively
1) Demonstrate Commitment to Integrity and Ethical Values	No	Ineffective
2) Exercise Oversight Responsibility	Yes	Effective with internal control deficiencies and compensating controls noted
3) Establish Structure, Responsibility and Authority	Yes	Effective with internal control deficiencies and compensating controls noted

4) Demonstrate Commitment to Competence	Yes	Effective
5) Enforce Accountability	No	Ineffective

Component Evaluation		
Component	Designed & Implemented (Yes/No)	Operating Effectively
Control Environment	No	Ineffective

In the table above, management concludes the Control Environment Component is not designed, implemented, and operating effectively since two principles are not designed, implemented, and operating effectively due to the identified deficiencies from the summary log. Each principle supports the design, implementation, operational effectiveness of the associated component. If one principle is ineffective, management is unable to conclude that the component is effective.[10] In the table below, since management concluded that the Control Environment is not operating effectively, it must conclude that the overall system of internal control was not operating effectively and an entity-level control material weakness must be reported.

Table 5 Overall Assessment of a System of Internal Control

Overall Assessment of a System of Internal Control		
System Evaluation	Designed & Implemented (Yes/No)	Operating Effectively
Control Environment	No	Ineffective
Risk Assessment	Yes	Effective
Control Activities	Yes	Effective
Information and Communication	Yes	Effective
Monitoring	Yes	Effective
Are all Components operating together in an integrated manner?	No	Ineffective

Overall Evaluation of a System of Internal Control	
Overall Evaluation	Operating Effectively
Is the overall system of internal control effective?	No

---

[10] See Green Book OV3.03, Factors of Effective Internal Control

V. CORRECTING INTERNAL CONTROL DEFICIENCIES

A. Importance of Correcting Internal Control Deficiencies

Correcting control deficiencies is an integral part of management accountability and must be considered a priority by the Agency. An Agency's ability to correct control deficiencies is an indicator of the strength of its internal control environment. Effective remediation of control deficiencies is essential to achieving the objectives of the FMFIA, and uncorrected or longstanding control deficiencies must be considered in determining the overall effectiveness of internal control. The corrective action process provides the mechanism for management to present a comprehensive plan for addressing the risk associated with a control deficiency.

B. Corrective Action Plan Requirements

Agencies should perform a root-cause analysis of the deficiency to ensure that subsequent strategies and plans address the root of the problem and not just the symptoms. Identifying and developing an understanding of the root cause of control deficiencies is management's responsibility. Management should incorporate IG and GAO audit findings as part of its identification process; however, auditors are not responsible for identifying root causes of control deficiencies. As a result, reliance on audit findings or recommendations alone may lead to incomplete corrective actions. Management should also consider alternative risk mitigation strategies and perform cost-benefit analysis to determine the best or most cost-effective solution.

A summary of the corrective action plans for material weaknesses that have not been fully mitigated at the time of reporting must be included in the Agency's AFR, PAR, or other management report. Also see Section VI for reporting on material weaknesses. The summary discussion must include a description of the material weakness, status of corrective actions, and timeline for resolution.

Management must maintain more thoroughly detailed corrective action plans internally, which must be made available for OMB and audit review. Management's process for resolution and corrective action of identified internal control deficiencies must:

- Communicate corrective actions to the appropriate level of the Agency and delegate authority for completing corrective actions to appropriate personnel.
- Determine the resources required to correct a control deficiency. The corrective action plan must indicate the types of resources needed (e.g., additional personnel, contract support, training, etc.), including non-financial resources, such as Senior Leadership support for correcting the control deficiency.
- Include critical path milestones that affect the overall schedule and performance of the corrective actions needed to resolve the control deficiency. Critical path milestones must lead to a date certain of the correction of the control deficiency.
- Require prompt resolution and internal control testing to validate the correction of the control deficiency.
- Ensure that accurate records of the status of the identified control deficiency are maintained and updated throughout the entire process.

- Ensure that the corrective action plans are consistent with laws, regulations, and Agency policy.
- Ensure that performance appraisals of appropriate officials reflect effectiveness in resolving or implementing corrective action for identified material weaknesses.
- Fully disclose uncorrected internal control weaknesses and highlight those that are material.

A determination that a control deficiency has been corrected should be made by the Senior Accountable Official only when sufficient corrective actions have been taken and validated. This determination must be in writing, supported by appropriate documentation, and made available for review by appropriate officials, e.g., the Agency's Senior Management Council or equivalent.

C. Audit Follow Up and Cooperative Audit Resolution and Oversight Initiatives

As managers consider Office of Inspectors General (OIG), GAO, and other investigative audit reports in identifying and correcting internal control deficiencies, they must be mindful of the statutory requirements included in the Inspector General Act, as amended, and OMB Circular No. A-50, *Audit Follow-up*. Management has a responsibility to complete action, in a timely manner, on audit recommendations on which agreement with the OIG has been reached. Management must make a decision regarding OIG audit recommendations within a six-month period after issuance of the audit report and implement management's decision within one year to the extent practicable.

Some agencies use cooperative audit resolution and oversight initiatives (CAROI)[11] to complement oversight of corrective actions and internal control efforts. In addition, the Uniform Grant Guidance encourages agencies to use cooperative audit resolution mechanisms as part of audit follow-up techniques that promote prompt corrective actions by improving communication, fostering collaboration, promoting trust, and developing a common understanding of audit findings to improve Federal program outcomes. The AGA has conducted research and has developed a framework to implement CAROI at Federal agencies. The AGA provides, "the CAROI is a tool for achieving: 1) alternative and creative approaches to resolving audit findings and their underlying causes, and 2) greater success in attaining program goals at all levels of government through the constructive use of monitoring and technical assistance (i.e., oversight activities)." While the establishment of a CAROI is not a requirement of this document, a CAROI or similar construct is encouraged.

---

[11] https://www.agacgfm.org/AGA/ToolsResources/documents/CAROI.pdf.

VI. REPORTING ON INTERNAL CONTROLS

A. Annual Assurance Statement.

The assurance statement and summary information related to Section 2 and Section 4 of the FMFIA must be provided in a single report section of the annual AFR, PAR, or other management report labeled "Analysis of Entity's Systems, Controls and Legal Compliance." The section must include the annual assurance statement, a summary of the Agency's process for assessing internal control effectiveness and resulting material weaknesses and corrective action plans as of September 30 of a given fiscal year.[12] The assurance statement is an accountability statement so only essential information must be included. Table 5 provides a summary of internal control reporting requirements, and Exhibits 1, 2, and 3 provide illustrative examples of assurance statements.

B. Reporting Pursuant to Integration of Enterprise Risk Management and Internal Control

Management has discretion in determining the scope of operations, reporting, and compliance objectives based on the Agency's risk profile as described in Section II of this document. Agencies are required to provide assurances on their process to identify risks and establish controls or integrate existing controls to the identified risk. Some of these internal control systems may have been operating effectively prior to integration of these risks. These assurances should be built out over time following a maturity model approach and reported in the AFR along with a report on identified material weaknesses and corrective actions. Until an Agency has fully implemented an ERM approach to risk management they may continue to provide the existing risk assurance statements to their OIG and/or private accounting firms.

C. Reporting Pursuant to OMB Circular No. A-123, Appendix A

Appendix A of OMB Circular No. A-123 provides a methodology for agency management to assess, document and report on internal controls over reporting. This document also encourages an integrated approach to assess the internal controls over reporting considering the current legislative and regulatory environment in which Federal entities operate. Management's assessment of internal control over external financial reporting must follow the assessment methodology provided in Appendix A to Circular No. A-123, *Internal Control Over Reporting*.

---

[12] Agencies may use roll forward procedures for timing differences in different types of internal control assessments (e.g., timing differences between June 30 and September 30).

D. Reporting Pursuant to OMB Circular No. A-130, Appendix I

Appendix I of OMB Circular No. A-130, *Responsibilities for Protecting and Managing Federal Information Resources*, establishes minimum requirements for Federal information security programs, assigns Federal Agency responsibilities for the security of information and information systems, and links Agency information security programs and Agency management control systems established in accordance with OMB Circular No. A-123. The appendix also establishes requirements for Federal privacy programs, assigns responsibilities for privacy program management, and describes how agencies must take a coordinated approach to implementing information security and privacy controls.

E. Reporting Pursuant to Section 2—31 U.S.C. 3512(d) (2)

Section 2-31 U.S.C 3512(d) (2), commonly referred to as Section 2 of the FMFIA requires that the head of each Executive Agency annually submit to the President and the Congress (i) a statement on whether there is reasonable assurance that the Agency's controls are achieving their intended objectives; and (ii) a report on material weaknesses in the Agency's controls.

- **Statement of Assurance.** The statement of assurance represents the Agency head's informed judgment as to the overall adequacy and effectiveness of internal control within the Agency related to operations, reporting, and compliance. The statement must take one of the following forms:
    - unmodified statement of assurance (no material weaknesses or lack of compliance reported);
    - modified statement of assurance, considering the exceptions explicitly noted (one or more material weaknesses or lack of compliance reported); or
    - statement of no assurance (no processes in place or pervasive material weaknesses).

In deciding on the type of assurance to provide, the Agency head should consider information from the assessment process described in Section IV of this Circular, with input from senior program and administrative officials. Management is precluded from concluding that the Agency's internal control is effective (unmodified statement of assurance) if there are one or more material weaknesses. In support of a single assurance statement, a detailed summary of management assurances must also be provided in the "Other Information" section of the annual AFR, PAR, or other management report. The detailed assurances should mirror the single assurance statement and provide assurance over the effectiveness of internal controls in each supporting area of operations, reporting (including external financial reporting), and compliance.

The Agency Head must sign the statement of assurance.

F. Reporting Pursuant to Section 4—31 U.S.C. 3512(d) (2) (B)

Section 4-31 U.S.C. 3512(d) (2) (B) commonly referred to as Section 4 of the FMFIA, requires CFO Act Agencies, a separate report on whether the Agency's financial management systems comply with government-wide requirements. These financial management systems requirements are mandated by Section 803 (a) of the Federal Financial Management Improvement Act and Appendix D to OMB Circular No. A-123, *Compliance with the Federal Financial Management Improvement Act of 1996*. FFMIA Section 803(a) requirements include compliance with Federal Financial Management System Requirements, applicable Federal accounting standards, and the United States Standard General Ledger (USSGL) at the transaction level. If the Agency's systems do not comply with financial systems requirements, the statement must list the lack of compliance noted and discuss the Agency's plans for bringing its systems into compliance. Financial management systems include both financial and financially-related (or mixed) systems.

G. Government Corporations

For government corporations, Section 306 of the Chief Financial Officers Act established a reporting requirement related to the internal controls for corporations covered by the Government Corporation Control Act. These corporations must submit an annual management report to the Congress. This report must include, among other items, a statement on control systems by the head of the management of the corporation consistent with the requirements of the FMFIA. The corporation is required to provide the President, the Director of OMB, and the Comptroller General a copy of the management report when it is submitted to the Congress.

H. Classified Matters

The statement of assurance is made available to the public. However, relevant information that is specifically prohibited from disclosure by any provision of law, or specifically required by Executive Order to protect the interest of national defense or the conduct of foreign affairs, must not be included in the statement made available to the public. Descriptions of major vulnerabilities must be framed in such a way as to preclude an adverse party from exploiting the information.

Table 6 Summary of OMB Circular No. A-123 Reporting Requirements

Category	Definition	Reporting
Control Deficiency	A control deficiency exists when the design, implementation, or operation of a control does not allow management or personnel, in the normal course of performing their assigned functions, to achieve control objectives and address related risks. [13] A deficiency in design exists when (1) a control necessary to meet a control objective is missing or (2) an existing control is not properly designed so that even if the control operates as designed, the control objective would not be met. [14] A deficiency in implementation exists when a properly designed control is not implemented correctly in the internal control system. [15] A deficiency in operation exists when a properly designed control does not operate as designed, or when the person performing the control does not possess the necessary authority or competence to perform the control effectively. [16]	Internal to the organization and not reported externally. Progress against corrective action plans must be periodically assessed and reported to agency management.
Significant Deficiency	A significant deficiency is a deficiency, or a combination of deficiencies, in internal control that is less severe than a material weakness yet important enough to merit attention by those charged with governance. [17]	Internal to the organization and not reported externally. Progress against corrective action plans must be periodically assessed and reported to agency management.

---

[13] Green Book OV3.08
[14] Green Book OV3.05
[15] Green Book OV3.05
[16] Green Book OV3.06
[17] Consistent with AU-C 260, *The Auditor's Communication With Those Charged With Governance*, the 2011 revision of *Government Auditing Standards* defines those charged with governance as the person(s) or organization(s) with responsibility for overseeing the strategic direction of the entity and the obligations related to the accountability of the entity. This includes overseeing the financial reporting process, subject matter, or program under audit, including related internal controls.

Category	Definition	Reporting
Material Weakness	A significant deficiency that the Agency Head determines to be significant enough to report outside of the Agency as a material weakness. In the context of the Green Book, non-achievement of a relevant principle and related component results in a material weakness.[18] A material weakness in internal control over operations might include, but is not limited to, conditions that: • impacts the operating effectiveness of Entity- Level Controls; • impairs fulfillment of essential operations or mission; • deprives the public of needed services; or • significantly weakens established safeguards against fraud, waste, loss, unauthorized use, or misappropriation of funds, property, other assets, or conflicts of interest. A material weakness in internal control over reporting is a significant deficiency, in which the Agency Head determines significant enough to impact internal or external decision-making and reports outside of the Agency as a material weakness. A material weakness in internal control over external financial reporting is a deficiency, or a combination of deficiencies, in internal control, such that there is a reasonable possibility[19] that a material misstatement of the entity's financial statements will not be prevented, or detected and corrected, on a timely basis. A material weakness in internal control over compliance is a condition where management lacks a process that reasonably ensures preventing a violation of law or regulation that has a direct and material effect on financial reporting or significant effect on other reporting or achieving Agency objectives.	Material weaknesses and a summary of corrective actions must be reported to OMB and Congress through the AFR, PAR, or other management reports. Progress against corrective action plans must be periodically assessed and reported to agency management.

Exhibit 1 Illustrative Unmodified Assurance Statement

The [Agency] management is responsible for managing risks and maintaining effective internal control to meet the objectives of Sections 2 and 4 of the Federal Managers' Financial Integrity Act. The [Agency] conducted its assessment of risk and internal control in accordance with OMB Circular No. A-123, *Management's Responsibility for Enterprise Risk Management and Internal Control*. Based on the results of the assessment, the Agency can provide reasonable assurance that internal control over operations, reporting, and compliance were operating effectively as of September 30, 20XX.

Head of the Agency Signature

Exhibit 2 Illustrative Modified Assurance Statement

The [Agency] management is responsible for managing risks and maintaining effective internal control to meet the objectives of Sections 2 and 4 of the Federal Managers' Financial Integrity Act. The [Agency] conducted its assessment of risk and internal control in accordance with OMB Circular No. A-123, *Management's Responsibility for Enterprise Risk Management and Internal Control*. Based on the results of the assessment, the Agency can provide reasonable assurance that internal control over operations, reporting, and compliance were operating effectively as of September 30, 20XX, except for the following material weaknesses reported:

- [Insert brief description of each internal control material weakness;]

Head of the Agency Signature

---

[18] The Federal Information Security Modernization Act of 2014 no longer requires that a significant deficiency identified be reported as a material weakness for FMFIA.

[19] In this definition, a reasonable possibility exists when the likelihood of the event is reasonably possible or probable as those terms are used in AU-C 265, *Communicating Internal Control Related Matters Identified in an Audit*.

Exhibit 3 Illustrative Statement of No Assurance

The [Agency] management is responsible for managing risks and maintaining effective internal control to meet the objectives of Sections 2 and 4 of the Federal Managers' Financial Integrity Act. The [Agency] conducted its assessment of risk and internal control in accordance with OMB Circular No. A-123, *Management's Responsibility for Enterprise Risk Management and Internal Control*. Based on the results of the assessment, the Agency is unable to provide assurance that internal control over operations, reporting, and compliance was operating effectively due to the following material weaknesses:

- [Insert brief description of each internal control material weakness;]

Head of the Agency Signature

I. Agencies Obtaining Audit Opinions on Internal Control

Agencies may be required or may at their choice elect to receive an audit opinion on internal control over external financial reporting. These Agencies must provide a separate assurance statement for internal control over external financial reporting. The Green Book and OMB Circular No. A-123 provide adequate criteria for management's assessment of internal control and related management assurances. Public Company Accounting Oversight Board requirements for the private sector are not requirements of the Federal Government.

VII. ADDITIONAL CONSIDERATIONS

A. Managing Privacy Risks in Federal Programs

The Federal Government necessarily creates, collects, uses, processes, stores, maintains, disseminates, discloses, and disposes of Personally Identifiable Information (PII) to carry out the missions mandated by Federal statute. The term PII, as defined by OMB, refers to information that can be used to distinguish or trace an individual's identity, either alone or when combined with other information that is linked or linkable to a specific individual. Because there are many different types of information that can be used to distinguish or trace an individual's identity, the term PII is necessarily broad. To determine whether information is PII, the agency must perform an assessment of the specific risk that an individual can be identified using the information with other information that is linked or linkable to the individual. In performing this assessment, it is important to recognize that information that is not PII can become PII whenever additional information becomes available – in any medium and from any source – that would make it possible to identify an individual.

Once the agency determines that an information system contains PII, the agency must then consider the privacy risks and the associated risk to agency operations, agency assets, individuals, other organizations, and the Nation. When considering privacy risks, the agency must consider the risks to an individual or individuals associated with the agency's creation, collection, use, processing, storage, maintenance, dissemination, disclosure, and disposal of their PII. In particular, the agency must evaluate the sensitivity of each individual data element that is PII, as well as all of the data elements together. The sensitivity level of the PII will depend on the context, including the purpose for which the PII is created, collected, used, processed, stored, maintained, disseminated, disclosed, or disposed. For example, the sensitivity level of a list of individuals' names may depend on the source of the information, the other information associated with the list, the intended use of the information, how the information will be processed and shared, and the ability to access the information. In addition, when determining the privacy and associated risks, the agency must also consider the volume of PII. A higher volume of PII about a single individual or multiple individuals may pose increased privacy or associated risks.

Agency Privacy Programs. In order to manage Federal information resources that involve PII, agencies must develop, implement, document, maintain, and oversee agency-wide privacy programs that include people, processes, and technologies. Agencies' privacy programs are led by the Senior Agency Official for Privacy (SAOP) and are responsible for ensuring compliance with applicable privacy requirements, developing and evaluating privacy policy, and managing privacy risks. Privacy programs' review of privacy risks should begin at the earliest planning and development stages of agency actions and policies that involve PII, and should continue throughout the life cycle of the information.

Privacy Impact Assessments. As a general matter, an agency must conduct a privacy impact assessment (PIA) under section 208(b) of the E-Government Act of 2002, absent an applicable exception under that section, when the agency develops, procures, or uses information technology to create, collect, use, process, store, maintain, disseminate, disclose, or dispose of PII.[20] A PIA is an analysis of how PII is handled to ensure that handling conforms to applicable privacy requirements, determine the privacy risks associated with an information system or activity, and evaluate ways to mitigate privacy risks. A PIA is both an analysis and a formal document detailing the process and the outcome of the analysis.

A PIA is one of the most valuable tools Federal agencies use to ensure compliance with applicable privacy requirements and manage privacy risks. Agencies must conduct and draft a PIA with sufficient clarity and specificity to demonstrate that the agency fully considered privacy and incorporated appropriate privacy protections from the earliest stages of the agency activity and throughout the information life cycle. In order to conduct a meaningful PIA, the agency's SAOP must work closely with the program managers, information system owners, information technology experts, security officials, counsel, and other relevant agency officials.

Moreover, a PIA is not a time-restricted activity that is limited to a particular milestone or stage of the information system or PII life cycles. Rather, the privacy analysis must continue throughout the information system and PII life cycles. Accordingly, a PIA must be considered a living document that agencies are required to update whenever changes to the information technology, changes to the agency's practices, or other factors alter the privacy risks associated with the use of such information technology.

In addition to serving as an important analytical tool for agencies, a PIA also serves as notice to the public regarding the agency's practices with respect to privacy and information technology. All PIAs must be drafted in plain language and must be posted on the agency's website, unless doing so would raise security concerns or reveal classified or sensitive information. Although PIAs are generally required by law, such as by the E-Government Act of 2002, agencies may also develop policies to require PIAs in circumstances where a PIA would not be required by law.

---

[20] *See* 44 U.S.C. § 3501 note. Section 208(b) of the E-Government Act requires agencies, absent an applicable exception under this section, to conduct a PIA before: (i) developing or procuring IT that collects, maintains, or disseminates information that is in an identifiable form; or (ii) initiating a new collection of information that – (I) will be collected, maintained, or disseminated using IT; and (II) includes any information in an identifiable form permitting the physical or online contacting of a specific individual, if identical questions have been posed to, or identical reporting requirements imposed on, 10 or more persons, other than agencies, instrumentalities, or employees of the Federal Government.

Risk Management Framework. Agencies' privacy programs have responsibilities under the Risk Management Framework.[21] The Risk Management Framework provides a disciplined and structured process that integrates information security, privacy, and risk management activities into the information system development life cycle. Agencies should refer to OMB Circular No. A-130 for more detailed guidance regarding the role of agencies' privacy programs under the Risk Management Framework.

B. Conducting Acquisition Assessments under OMB Circular No. A-123

In May 2008, OMB's Office of Federal Procurement Policy (OFPP) issued guidelines, including an assessment template, to (1) establish a standard approach for assessing acquisition activities and programs; and (2) integrate these efforts into existing agency internal control processes and practices required by OMB Circular No. A-123. The template was adopted from the Government Accountability Office (GAO) Framework for Assessing the Acquisition Function at Federal Agencies (Framework) (GAO-05-218G) and consists of four interrelated areas, i.e. cornerstones, that are essential to an efficient, effective and accountable acquisition process: (1) organizational alignment and leadership; (2) policies and processes; (3) human capital; and (4) information management and stewardship. Assessments conducted using this Acquisition Framework can continue to be leveraged in meeting the requirements of the current update to OMB Circular No. A-123.

These guidelines are based on GAO's Framework for Assessing the Acquisition Function at Federal Agencies (GAO-05-218G) and can continue to be leveraged in meeting the requirements of the current update to OMB Circular No. A-123. Each of the elements of OMB's Acquisition Framework is reviewed below in relation to the Green Book. The critical factors contained in each element of the acquisition framework are used where possible to depict these similarities and differences. The following illustrative table is included in setting out concepts that are common to both OMB's acquisition framework and the Green Book and required by the Green Book, but not part of the acquisition framework.

---

[21] Traditionally, the Risk Management Framework was a framework to help agencies address information security and related risks in the authorization process for Federal information systems. NIST has published a suite of standards and guidelines that describe how to implement an agency-wide risk management framework. As of the date of this publication, many of the existing NIST standards and guidelines that detail how to implement an agency-wide risk management framework do not fully address the role of privacy and agencies' privacy programs. In the future, NIST may revise or develop standards and guidelines to further clarify how privacy and agencies' privacy programs are integrated into the Risk Management Framework.

Table 7 Comparison of OMB Acquisition Framework and GAO Green Book

Common to Both	Differences Required by the Green Book
• Aligning Acquisition with Agency Mission and Needs • Commitment from Leadership	None
• Planning Strategically • Effectively Managing the Acquisition Process • Promoting Successful Outcomes of Major Projects	Management Responsibility for considering Fraud Risks
• Valuing and Investing in the Acquisition Workforce • Strategic Human Capital Planning • Acquiring, Developing, and Retaining Talent • Creating Results-Oriented Organizational Cultures	Management Responsibility for considering Fraud Risks
• Identify Data and Technology that Support Acquisition Management Decisions • Safeguarding the Integrity of Operations and Data	None

Agencies should continue their prior assessment activities under the acquisition framework to comply with the 2014 revision of the Green Book. For example, the framework describes the Commitment from Leadership element to include management providing clear, strong and ethical executive leadership, and effective communication, and continuous improvement. These activities align with the Green Book principles that require an entity to demonstrate commitment to integrity and ethical values, while ensuring that management should communicate the necessary quality information both internally and externally.

One required Green Book principle that is absent from the current acquisition framework is management's consideration for potential fraud when identifying, analyzing and responding to risks. Agencies must consider fraud risks in their strategic plans, and ensure agency professionals involved in planning for, reviewing, awarding, and managing deliverables under contract and throughout the acquisition lifecycle receive training on fraud indicators and risks. Additional guidance covering administrative actions and procedures for preventing fraud in emergency responses and contingency operations can be found in OMB's emergency acquisitions guide[22] and in the Federal Acquisition Regulation (FAR).

C. Managing Grants Risks in Federal Programs

On December 26, 2013, OMB published the final guidance, *Uniform Administrative Requirements, Cost Principles, and Audit Requirements for Federal Awards* ("Uniform Guidance") 2 CFR 200. These new requirements set forth standards for obtaining consistency and uniformity among Federal agencies for the audit of non-Federal entities expending Federal awards. The requirements seek to effectively focus Federal resources, improve Federal grant

---

[22] Memorandum for Chief Acquisition Officers Senior Procurement Executives. Emergency Acquisitions Guide 1/14/2011. http://www.whitehouse.gov/omb/procurement

award performance, and create a government-wide framework for ensuring effective fiscal management of Federal grants. In addition, the requirements in 2 CFR 200.501, Audit Requirements, reduce the administrative burden on recipients by increasing the single audit threshold to $750,000 in Federal award expenditures per year. The guidance in 2 CFR 200.205 requires Federal awarding agency review of risk(s) posed by applicants, risk evaluation(s) whenever making new awards, and authorized use of a risk based approach.

Within each Federal Agency, there is a shared interest for management and oversight of Federal grant dollars from both a financial management and grants management perspective. Leveraging the risk-based perspective, the internal controls framework should serve as a mechanism to ensure effective and efficient allocation and use of Federal grant dollars. Agencies must consider fraud risks in their strategic plans and ensure Federal officials involved in planning for, awarding, and managing grants and other forms of financial assistance receive training of fraud indicators and risk.

In addition, the Federal Government has a number of complex inter-dependencies with State and local governments, and other recipients of Federal funding. From an ERM perspective, these inter-dependencies are called the "extended enterprise" impacts the Agency's risk management, and give rise to certain additional risks, which need to be considered in the Agency's risk profile. Finally, ERM and use of data analytics is an emerging best practice; examples include:

- **Pre-award Decision Support:** Appropriate tools and data analytics made available to Federal awarding agencies to properly conduct risk analysis.

- **Pre/Post Award Monitoring Plans and Activities:** Federal awarding agencies use of relevant data to determine risks and take appropriate action prior to making awards.

- **Award Grantee Risk Mitigation:** Federal awarding agencies plan for and execute monitoring and mitigation activities meeting their specific needs.

- **Grant Policy Monitoring Standards:** Federal awarding agencies manage grant portfolios using a common set of risk-based standards.

D. Managing Antideficiency Act Risks

The Antideficiency Act (ADA) imposes restrictions on the amounts of obligations or expenditures that agencies may make. ADA violations are ultimately reported to the President, Congress, and the Government Accountability Office. An ADA violation may be a symptom of an underlying control deficiency. OMB Circular No. A-11, Section 150, Administrative Control of Funds outlines requirements for the administrative control of funds under the ADA. Section 150.3 explains the relationship between an agency's internal controls and its fund controls. In addition, OMB Circular No. A-11, Section 145, Requirements for Reporting Antideficiency Act

Violations, provides more information about the ADA, and also provides agencies with guidelines for reporting violations. The Agency's risk profile as described in Section II must include a review of the agency's budget authority, from sources such as appropriations legislation, and identify any areas in which there is a risk of violating the ADA.